DECADES OF THE
20TH
CENTURY

1990s

ELDORADO INK

DECADES OF THE 20TH CENTURY

1900s

1910s

1920s

1930s

1940s

1950s

1960s

1970s

1980s

1990s

DECADES OF THE
20ᵀᴴ CENTURY

1990s

ELDORADO INK

Published by Eldorado Ink
2099 Lost Oak Trail
Prescott, AZ 86303
www.eldoradoink.com

Milan Bobek, Editor
Judith C. Callomon, Historical consultant
Samuel J. Patti, Consulting editor

Printed and bound in Slovenia

Publisher Cataloging Data

1990s / [Milan Bobek, editor].
    p. cm. -- (Decades of the 20th century)
    Includes index.
    Summary: This volume, arranged chronologically, presents key events that have shaped the decade, from significant political occurrences to details of daily life.
    ISBN 1-932904-09-3
    1. Nineteen nineties   2. History, Modern--20th century--Chronology   3. History, Modern--20th century--Pictorial works
I. Bobek, Milan   II. Title: Nineteen nineties   III. Series
    909.82/9--dc22

Picture research and photography by Anne Hobart Lang and Rolf Lang of AHL Archives. Additional research by Heritage Picture Collection, London.

CONTENTS

INTO THE NEW MILLENNIUM

In the 1990s, the political map is redrawn. The Soviet Union crumbles and more than 70 years of Soviet communism come to an end, leaving the United States as the solitary superpower. The collapse of Communism in Eastern Europe exposes ethnic tensions and war breaks out in the Balkans. However, in South Africa the oppressive apartheid system is finally dismantled. Peace also comes to war-torn Central America. In the world of science, distant planets such as Venus and Mercury are mapped.

OPPOSITE: Firefighters in the burning Kuwaiti oil fields during the Gulf War of 1991.

1990–1999

KEY EVENTS OF THE DECADE

- SOVIET UNION COLLAPSES
- GULF WAR
- APARTHEID ENDS
- YUGOSLAVIA BREAKS UP
- U.N. EARTH SUMMIT
- WAR IN BOSNIA
- RWANDAN CIVIL WAR
- DEATH OF PRINCESS DIANA
- COLLAPSE OF ASIAN ECONOMIES

- HALE-BOPP COMET
- HUBBLE SPACE TELESCOPE LAUNCHED
- PLANET VENUS IS MAPPED
- CLONING TAKES OFF
- ANIMATRONICS COME TO CINEMA
- CENTENARY OLYMPIC GAMES
- SINGLE EUROPEAN CURRENCY

WORLD POPULATION **5,295** MILLION

GERMANY UNITES, MANDELA IS FREED

ANC leader Nelson Mandela is released from prison after 27 years in captivity. Iraq invades Kuwait, prompting an immediate response from the United Nations and the United States. Tension rises as U.S. forces mass on the Saudi Arabian border. East and West Germany are finally united. The Soviet Union begins to crumble as Lithuania declares independence. The Hubble Space Telescope is launched but proves to be defective. A new hand-held computer game console goes on sale.

1990

Jan	4	Former Panama leader Manuel Noriega is charged in Miami with drug trafficking
Feb	2	President F.W. de Klerk ends a 20 year ban on the ANC
	11	Nelson Mandela is released after 27 years of imprisonment
	21	Namibia becomes an independent state
	25	U.S. backed Violeta Chamorro wins Nicaraguan elections
Mar	11	Lithuania declares independence from the Soviet Union
Apr	24	Hubble Space Telescope is launched into orbit
May	29	Boris Yeltsin is elected president of the Russian Federation
June	12	Russian Federation declares itself a sovereign state
July	19	Iraqi troops mass on the Kuwaiti border
Aug	2	Iraqi forces invade Kuwait. Emir flees to Saudi Arabia
	6	U.N. Security Council imposes sanctions against Iraq
	24	Hostage Brian Keenan, held in Lebanon since 1986, is released
Sep	28	Serbian parliament strips Kosovo of autonomy in Yugoslavia
Oct	2	East and West Germany are reunited
Dec	9	Slobodan Milosevic is elected the president of Serbia in the country's first free elections in 50 years

MANDELA FREED

The South African government under President de Klerk (b. 1936) lifts the ban on the African National Congress (ANC) and other anti-apartheid parties and frees ANC leader Nelson Mandela after 27 years in prison. Talks begin on moving South Africa towards multiracial democracy.

NAMIBIA INDEPENDENT

The last white-run colony in Africa gains its independence as South Africa relinquishes its hold on South West Africa, renamed Namibia. The former German colony had been administered by South Africa since 1919 under League of Nations and U.N. mandates. Sam Nujoma (b. 1929), the leader of the SWAPO opposition, is elected president.

IRAQ INVADES KUWAIT

Iraq invades the neighboring oil-rich sheikdom of Kuwait. The Emir flees to Saudi Arabia. Iraq's unprovoked invasion and potential threat to Saudi Arabia prompt an almost immediate reaction. The United Nations declares sanctions against Iraq and, in Operation Desert Shield, the United States airlifts 2,300 troops to Saudi Arabia within 18 hours. Iraqi leader Saddam Hussein (b. 1937) makes a formal peace treaty with long-term enemy Iran.

GERMANY UNITED

East and West Germany are reunited after pro-unity parties in East Germany win a majority in elections held in March and open talks with West Germany. In July, the government cedes sovereignty over economic, monetary, and social policy to West Germany. The Deutschmark becomes the official currency. Elections held across Germany in December return Christian Democrat Helmut Kohl to power.

ABOVE: Free at last, ANC leader Nelson Mandela meets President George Bush in the White House.

THE EUROPEAN

A new concept in journalism, *The European*, is founded as an English-language newspaper, dealing with news from a European perspective. It will not be successful.

POSSESSION

British writer A.S. Byatt (b. 1938) has published what is her best novel. Full of symbols and symmetries, it recreates the Victorian world (and writings) of the biographers' subject as well as their obsession with, and possession of, their quarry.

ABOVE: Hubble Space Telescope deployed from space shuttle *Discovery*.

ABOVE: Martina Navratilova takes the Pilkington Glass Ladies Singles Trophy at Eastbourne, England, as an appetizer for her Wimbledon triumph a month later.

BURMESE ELECTIONS
The National League for Democracy wins multiparty elections in Burma but the army refuses to hand over power. The League's co-founder is Aung San Suu Kyi (b. 1945), who has been under house arrest since 1989 because of her opposition to the ruling military junta. She is awarded the Nobel Peace Prize in 1991.

NICARAGUAN ELECTIONS
Elections held in Nicaragua are won by U.S.-backed Violeta Barrios de Chamorro. A month later the United States lifts sanctions and by the end of June the Contras are disbanded. In 1991, U.S. president Bush pledges economic support for Nicaragua. The cost to Nicaragua of economic sanctions and the Contra war is estimated at $15 billion, with some 30,000 people killed.

NEWS FROM NEPTUNE
U.S. space probe *Voyager 2* flies within 3,000 miles of Neptune, reporting four rings, six new moons, and a stormy surface like that of Jupiter.

GAME BOY
Japanese computer manufacturer Nintendo launch Game Boy, the first programmable hand-held computer games console. It is an instant success.

BACK TO EARTH
Space shuttle *Columbia* returns to Earth after six days in orbit. It returns the Long Duration Exposure Facility, a railroad car-sized container of scientific experiments.

STRETCHABLE CERAMICS
Japanese researchers announce the development of ceramics that can be stretched at temperatures of about 2,912° F during manufacturing.

HUBBLE DEFECTIVE
The Hubble Space Telescope is launched by space shuttle *Discovery* from Kennedy Space Center. Orbiting at an altitude of 375 miles above the Earth, it is designed to see further into space than any Earthbound telescope. However, its main mirror is found to be flawed, distorting the images and limiting the telescope's usefulness.

SUCCESS FOR NAVRATILOVA
Czech-born American tennis star Martina Navratilova becomes queen of Wimbledon when she achieves her ninth singles title. She beats American player Zina Garrison in the final.

GERMANY WINS WORLD CUP
Defending champions Argentina scratch and fight to reach the final in Rome at the 14th soccer World Cup but lose a disappointing match to Germany.

ABOVE: American composer Aaron Copeland (b. 1900) dies. He is best known for his ballet *Appalachian Spring* (1944).

ABOVE: In the White House, the States and Russia agree to terms laying down the foundations for a future arms limitation agreement.

BELOW: A helicopter gunship covers the USS *Dwight D. Eisenhower* as she sails through the Suez Canal to the Mediterranean.

THE SOVIET UNION COLLAPSES

The Warsaw Pact is dissolved. A Communist coup takes place in the Soviet Union. Boris Yeltsin comes to power. Mikhail Gorbachev resigns as leader of the Soviet Union. The U.S.S.R. comes to an end 74 years after the Russian Revolution. Operation Desert Storm launches the Gulf War and a U.S. led multinational operation liberates Kuwait from Iraqi occupation. Croatia and Slovenia declare independence and Yugoslavia begins to break up.

OPPOSITE: Iraqi forces set fire to oil wells outside Kuwait City as they retreat from the region.

1991

Jan	**15**	Iraq fails to meet U.N. deadline for withdrawal from Kuwait
	16	Operation Desert Storm begins. U.S. led operation begins air offensive to liberate Kuwait
	18	Iraq sends Scud missiles against Israel
Feb	**17**	Serbia suspends provisional Kosovo constitution
	22	Retreating Iraqi forces torch Kuwaiti oil wells
	24	U.S. led troops begin ground offensive against Iraqi forces
	28	The Gulf War ends after Kuwait has been liberated
Apr	**30**	Kurdish refugees move into "safe havens"
May	**28**	Ethiopian People's Revolutionary Democratic Front captures Addis Ababa
May	**31**	Civil war ends in Angola
June	**17**	Population Registration Act ends apartheid in South Africa
	25	Republics of Croatia and Slovenia declare independence
July	**31**	U.S. president Bush and Soviet leader Gorbachev sign the Strategic Arms Reduction Treaty (START) to reduce the numbers of long-range nuclear weapons
Aug	**19**	Hard-line Communists stage coup against Soviet leader Mikhail Gorbachev
Oct	**15**	Clarence Thomas is confirmed to the Supreme Court
Dec	**25**	Mikhail Gorbachev resigns and the U.S.S.R. comes to an end

U.S.S.R. CRUMBLES

As Soviet control is removed from eastern Germany, the Warsaw Pact is formally dissolved. Inside the Soviet Union, Latvia and Estonia vote in referenda for independence, following the lead set by Lithuania. The U.S.S.R. continues to fall apart as domestic, economic, and political pressures mount. In August, hard-line Communists seize power while President Gorbachev is on holiday. The coup fails as Boris Yeltsin, president of Russia, leads popular resistance against it. As a result, Gorbachev's hold on power is seriously weakened and Ukraine and other states push for independence from the U.S.S.R. In December, Russia, Belarus, and Ukraine set up the Commonwealth of Independent States (CIS). The U.S.S.R. collapses and Gorbachev resigns on Christmas Day, bringing Communist Party rule and the Soviet Union to an end.

AIDS

The announcement that U.S. sports star Magic Johnson is HIV positive and the death from AIDS of British rock singer Freddie Mercury increase public awareness of the rapid worldwide spread of AIDS.

GULF WAR

In January, the United States leads allied forces in an air attack, code-named Operation Desert Thunder, against Saddam Hussein's capital in Baghdad, Iraq. Following a month of intensive bombing, ground forces begin to liberate Kuwait in February, achieving their objective within four days and driving Iraqi forces out of Kuwait. During the retreat, oil wells are torched, causing serious pollution. At the end of the war, allied casualties are 95 killed and 370 wounded. The Iraqis suffered 30,000 killed in air attacks. In the ground war, they lost 20,000 prisoners with 270 tanks destroyed.

ASTEROID PHOTOGRAPHED

The *Galileo* space probe passes within 995 miles of the asteroid Gaspra and photographs it. This is the first asteroid photograph ever taken in space.

PREHISTORIC REMAINS

The preserved body of a man who died around 3300 B.C. is found in a glacier in the Austrian Alps. Probably a hunter, he is tattooed on his back, knees, and ankles, and has a bow and a quiver of arrows.

ABOVE: A submarine bomb disposal expert attaches an explosive charge to an Iraqi mine in the Persian Gulf during the Gulf War.

ABOVE: An F-117A stealth fighter aircraft of the 37th Tactical Fighter Wing rolls towards the runway for the flight back home after Operation Desert Storm.

ABOVE: Demolished vehicles line Highway 8, the route that fleeing Iraqi forces took as they retreated from Kuwait.

ABOVE: Haitians, who had fled during the U.S. invasion, are repatriated and return home to their villages.

ABOVE: General "Stormin'" Norman Schwartzkopf, commander-in-chief, speaks to soldiers during Operation Desert Shield.

ABOVE: General Colin Powell consults the Pentagon while visiting troops during Operation Desert Shield.

APARTHEID ENDS

In February, President de Klerk announces plans to repeal all apartheid laws in South Africa. Legislation is passed to end racial controls on land ownership and in June, all remaining discriminatory laws are repealed. The United States ends sanctions against South Africa, and the country is readmitted into world sport.

ETHIOPIA AND SOMALIA

After a lengthy civil war, President Mengistu flees Ethiopia as 17 years of Marxist rule are brought to an end. Neighboring Somalia, meanwhile, collapses into anarchy as rival warlords fight for control following the overthrow of President Siyad Barrah in January.

JFK

A new film has been released about U.S. president Kennedy and the conspiracy theory surrounding his assassination. Directed by U.S. film director Oliver Stone (b. 1946), it stars American actor Kevin Costner (b. 1955) as the New Orleans district attorney.

MAPPING VENUS

While orbiting Venus, the U.S. unmanned spacecraft *Magellan* compiles a map of the surface by using radar signals.

POWELL OVERTAKES BEAMON

U.S. long jumper Mike Powell beats Bob Beamon's famous leap of 29 feet 2½ inches by 1½ inches at the World Athletics Championships in Tokyo. The world record had stood since the 1968 Olympics.

NATURAL DISASTERS

In April, a typhoon traveling at 145 miles per hour, strikes Bangladesh, killing more than 139,000 people and making ten million homeless. In June, Mt. Pinatubo, a Philippine volcano dormant for six hundred years, erupts and kills more than seven hundred people.

CONFLICT IN YUGOSLAVIA

The delicate balance between Catholic, Muslim, and Orthodox ethnic groups that held together under the tough rule of President Tito is now unraveling. Ethnic tensions between the different communities are rising and Yugoslavia is falling apart as Slovenia and Croatia declare their independence, exacerbated by newly elected Serbian leader Slobodan Milosevic (b. 1941) who is emphasizing ethnic differences to consolidate his power base. The Serb-dominated Yugoslav National Army (JNA) tries to prevent the breakup of the country and attacks Croatia, starting a lengthy and bitter war between the two states.

THE SILENCE OF THE LAMBS

Welsh actor Anthony Hopkins (b. 1937) plays Hannibal Lecter, psychiatrist turned serial killer, in a new film, *The Silence of the Lambs*, which has opened this year. U.S. film star Jodie Foster (b. 1962) plays an agent of the Federal Bureau of Investigation. A chilling movie, the horror is tightly controlled by director Jonathan Demme.

YUGOSLAVIA CRUMBLES AND LOS ANGELES BURNS

Interracial war breaks out in former Yugoslavia and the abhorrent term "ethnic cleansing" enters the language as evidence is televised of death camps in Bosnia. Race riots erupt in Los Angeles after the savage beating of a young black motorist. Elsewhere, the U.N. Earth Summit meets in Rio de Janeiro to discuss the future of planet Earth, Disneyland comes to Europe, and Expo 92 is held in Spain.

1992

Feb	1	U.N. negotiated peace comes into effect in El Salvador
	8	Winter Olympics open in France
	10	Alex Haley, the author of *Roots*, dies at the age of 70
Mar	1	Bosnia-Herzegovina declares independence following referendum
	2	Violence breaks out in Sarajevo between Serbs, Croats, and Muslims
	22	Communist rule ends in Albania after 45 years
Apr	16	Mujaheddin rebels take control in Afghanistan
	29	All-white jury acquits police of beating black American Rodney King
May	5	Serb and federal army forces begin bombardment of Sarajevo as violence escalates in Bosnia
Jun	29	The President of Algeria, Mohammed Boudiaf, is shot and killed at a political rally
July	25	Olympic Games open in Barcelona
Aug	12	North American Free Trade Agreement (NAFTA) between U.S., Canada, and Mexico, is created
	13	United Nations condemns Serbian policy of so-called "ethnic cleansing," describing it as a war crime
Sep	12	Actor Anthony Perkins dies at the age of 60
	25	New canal links Main and Danube rivers in Germany
Nov	3	Democrat Bill Clinton wins the U.S. presidential election defeating incumbent George H.W. Bush

ABOVE: The U.N. Commissioner for Refugees, Sadako Ogata, visits refugees returning to Somalia after the civil war.

WAR IN BOSNIA

After the former Yugoslav province of Bosnia votes for independence, a vicious war erupts. Croatia and Serbia attempt to carve up Bosnia along ethnic lines, threatening its multiracial nature in a campaign known as "ethnic cleansing." Bosnian Serbs backed by the Yugoslav National Army attack the fledgling country, which they wish to remain part of Greater Serbia. They overrun 70 percent of the country and set up a Serb government in Pale. In August, evidence emerges of Serbian death camps where Bosnian prisoners are kept in appalling conditions.

MUJAHEDDIN VICTORIOUS

Mujaheddin rebels in Afghanistan take control after a lengthy civil war, overthrowing the Communist government of President Najibullah. The Mujaheddin led the resistance to the Soviet occupation of the country from 1979–1989, and fought on to remove the Communist government.

L.A. RACE RIOTS

Race riots erupt in Los Angeles after police officers, who savagely beat a young black man, Rodney King, and are witnessed on video, are acquitted by an all-white jury. The verdict outrages the black community and reveals the extent of racial discrimination still experienced by many Americans.

CLINTON WINS ELECTION

Bill Clinton (b. 1946) from Arkansas wins the presidential election for the Democrats, only the second time in 24 years that a Democrat has gained the White House. However, Clinton's record of draft-dodging and marital infidelity infuriates right-wing Republicans, who campaign incessantly against him and his government.

LAST EUROPEAN COMMUNIST GOVERNMENT

In Albania, the last Communist government in Europe ends after the opposition Democrat Party wins a majority in the general election.

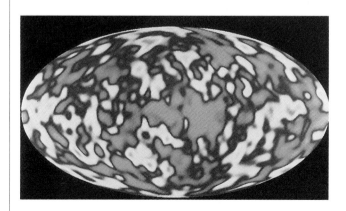

ABOVE: A microwave map of the whole sky compiled from a year's worth of data from NASA's Cosmic Background Explorer.

OPERATION RESTORE HOPE

In Somalia, United Nations military observers arrive in the capital Mogadishu to help distribute food aid. In what is code named Operation Restore Hope, some 17,000 soldiers drawn from the United States and ten other U.N. countries attempt to impose order to allow relief to be distributed. In a raid by U.S. Rangers to capture the Somali warlord Mohammad Farrah Aidid in October 1993, 18 soldiers are killed and 73 wounded.

EL SALVADOR

The United Nations finally brokers peace in El Salvador. The FMLN is granted the status of a political party. Peace talks began in 1990. It is estimated that about 100,000 people died in El Salvador between 1979 and 1990.

ABOVE: Riots and fires in Los Angeles follow after black motorist Rodney King was beaten by the LAPD.

LEFT: Democratic Presidential candidate Bill Clinton campaigns in Albuquerque, New Mexico, a key state in the election battle.

PERUVIAN GUERRILLA WAR

In Peru, Maoist leader Dr. Renoso Guzman is captured by the Army and police special forces, bringing an end to the activities of the Shining Path. The campaign of bombings, assassination, and terror has caused the deaths of more than 23,000 men and women since it began in 1982.

EXPO 92 IN SEVILLE

In April, Expo 92, the first Exposition Universelle for 22 years, opens in Seville, Spain. Nations from around the world display their innovations and achievements in industry, science, and the arts. One of the lasting monuments will be Alamillo Bridge. Designed by Spanish architect and civil engineer Santiago Calatrava, it is one of the most beautiful of all modern bridges. Its harp-like, cabled construction makes it an instant success.

GENETICALLY ENGINEERED WHEAT

U.S. biologists report in June that they have developed the first genetically engineered wheat, which is resistant to powerful herbicides.

WATER LINK

In Germany, a new canal opens linking the Main and Danube rivers. This completes a river and canal trade route from the Baltic Sea to the Black Sea.

DISNEYLAND COMES TO PARIS
Disneyland comes to Europe and the whole Disney culture, from the themed worlds to the cavalcades of wandering Disney characters brought to life, is transported to Paris.

SATELLITE CAPTURED
Three astronauts aboard the space shuttle *Endeavor* do a space walk to capture *Intelsat 6*, a communications satellite which has drifted into the wrong orbit. They put it back into the correct orbit.

BIG BANG NEWS
NASA scientists announce that their Cosmic Background Explorer (COBE) satellite, launched in 1989, has detected 15 billion year old clouds of matter that relate to the Big Bang. American astrophysicist George Fitzgerald Smoot (b. 1945), who heads COBE's team of analysts, announces that the satellite had found fluctuations in the background radiation, preserved from about 300,000 years after the Big Bang. The variations gave rise to stars, galaxies, and other cosmic structures.

ANTI-COLUMBUS DEMONSTRATIONS
Demonstrations against the celebrations of the 500th anniversary of the arrival of Christopher Columbus in the New World take place in many Latin American countries.

METHANE UNDER THE OCEAN
U.S. scientists find deposits of methane hydrate off the coast of northern North America, which may prove to be a huge source of natural gas.

EARTH SUMMIT
In June, representatives from 178 counties meet in an "Earth Summit," the U.N. Conference on Environment and Development, in Rio de Janeiro, Brazil. Most agree to phase out CFC gases, which cause depletion of the ozone layer, to preserve forests and protect biodiversity.

WOMEN PRIESTS
The Church of England Synod votes to allow women to be ordained as priests. Ten women were ordained to the Anglican priesthood in Australia during this year.

WINTER OLYMPICS
Twelve sites around Albertville in France are the venue for the 16th Winter Olympics. Short-track speed skating and freestyle moguls skiing become Olympic events. Sixteen year old Toni Nieminen takes ski jumping gold on the big hill and bronze on the small hill.

OLYMPIC GAMES
The emphasis returns to athletics at the 25th Olympic Games in Barcelona, Spain. In the long jump, U.S. athlete Carl Lewis (b. 1961) wins a gold for the third successive Games, while Vitali Sherb, of a post-Soviet Union team, dominates men's gymnastics. The American basketball "Dream Team" sweeps all before it.

ABOVE: Astronauts Hieb, Akers, and Thuot reel in the *Intelsat 6* satellite as part of the nine day STS-49 Mission.

ISRAEL AND PLO SIGN FOR PEACE

Israel and the PLO sign an historic peace accord. In Russia, the army crushes an attempted coup against Yeltsin's government. The European single market comes into force. Aborigines finally achieve recognition of their land rights in Australia. Explorers cross Antarctica on foot. New Zealander Jane Campion becomes the first woman film director to win the Palme d'Or and Spielberg's film *Schindler's List* opens to critical acclaim.

1993

Jan	1	EU's single market comes into force
	1	Czechoslovakia divides
Feb	26	World Trade Center bombed
Mar	17	Ballet star Rudolf Nureyev dies at age 55
May	24	Eritrea gains independence
Sep	13	PLO and Israel sign a peace agreement
Oct	4	Army crushes a potential coup in Moscow
	15	Nelson Mandela and President de Klerk jointly win Nobel Peace Prize
Nov	1	Maastricht Treaty comes into force creating the European Union
Dec	22	Aborigines win land rights in Australia

MIDDLE EAST PEACE ACCORD

In Washington, D.C., Prime Minister Rabin of Israel and the Palestine Liberation Organization (PLO) leader Yasser Arafat sign a treaty handing over control of the Gaza Strip and the West Bank city of Jericho to the Palestinians. Secret talks between the two sides in the Norwegian capital of Oslo have led to this historic agreement, which is designed to be the first stage in the gradual handing over of Israeli occupied territory to the Palestinians in return for their recognition of the state of Israel.

SINGLE EUROPEAN MARKET

The European single market comes into force, removing all obstacles to the free movement of trade, services, and people throughout the European Community. The Maastricht Treaty, establishing a single currency by 1999, comes into force and the European Community (EC) becomes the European Union (EU).

LANDMARK SPIELBERGS

U.S. film director Steven Spielberg has released two remarkable but highly contrasting movies. His *Jurassic Park* involves genetically recreated dinosaurs that run amok in the theme park to end all theme parks and is a commercial coup. More somber is *Schindler's List*. Based on Thomas Keneally's book *Schindler's Ark* and shot almost entirely in black and white, this moving film is concerned with the Holocaust and is Spielberg's account of Oskar Schindler, the German businessman who rescued Jews from the death camps by employing them in his factory. Liam Neeson (b. 1952) stars as Schindler. An epilogue shows actual survivors and Schindler's widow at his grave in Israel.

CZECHOSLOVAKIA DIVIDES

Following the success of pro-independence parties in Slovakia, Czechoslovakia splits amicably in two, with both the Czech Republic and Slovakia becoming independent states.

COMMUNIST COUP FAILS

A hard-line Communist coup against the Russian government of Boris Yeltsin is crushed when the army storms the White House, the parliament building in Moscow. The coup reveals levels of discontent in Russia caused by the failure of economic reforms.

ANOTHER SUPERNOVA

Spanish astronomer Francisco García announces that he has discovered another supernova (exploding star), some 11 million light years away.

ABOVE: Rudolph Nureyev, probably the best known ballet dancer of his generation, dies in Paris. He is seen here dancing in the States.

RUDOLF HAMETOVICH NUREYEV (1938–1993)

The great Russian ballet dancer Rudolf Nureyev has died in Paris of an AIDS related disease. In 1961, Nureyev defected from the Kirov Ballet while visiting Paris and in 1962 made his debut at Covent Garden with the great ballerina Margot Fonteyn. They formed a partnership that transformed ballet. From 1983 to 1989 Nureyev was artistic director to the Paris Opera. As a solo dancer he performed with the world's greatest companies.

ABOVE: U.S. Marines take part in the multinational relief effort Operation Restore Hope in Mogadishu, Somalia.

WAR IN BOSNIA
U.N. forces are deployed as peacekeepers in war-torn Bosnia. However, Bosnian Serbs continue to shell the regional capital of Sarajevo. Croatian forces shell the town of Mostar.

FRANCIS VINCENT (FRANK) ZAPPA (1940–1993)

American rock musician Frank Zappa has died after a two year battle with prostate cancer. Always at the forefront of experimental rock as guitarist, singer, and music writer, Zappa founded the group Mothers of Invention in the 1960s. Their first album *Freak Out!* was released in 1966. Zappa's first solo album was *Lumpy Gravy* (1968) and his final album *Yellow Shark*, appeared this year.

FIRST WOMAN ATTORNEY GENERAL
Janet Reno (b. 1938) becomes the first woman attorney general of the United States. The start of her new career is marred by a disaster during which more than 70 members of a cult religion die at Waco, Texas, while being besieged by the FBI.

"DON'T ASK, DON'T TELL"
President Clinton reaches an agreement with the Department of Defense whereby gays can serve in the military provided that they neither openly declare their homosexuality nor engage in homosexual activity.

FERMAT'S LAST THEOREM
British mathematician Andrew Wiles claims to have proved Fermat's Last Theorem. It is a mathematical proposition put forward in 1627 by Pierre de Fermat who omitted proving the theory.

5,000 MILE TELESCOPE
In August the Very Long Baseline Array, a collection of huge radio telescope dishes at ten different sites scattered over 5,000 miles, begins operation.

HUBBLE CORRECTED
During five spacewalks, astronauts aboard the space shuttle *Endeavor* "capture" the Hubble Space Telescope, correct its faults, and update it.

ROMANOVS FINGERPRINTED
Genetic material from the British relatives of the Romanovs, the last Russian Csars, are compared with material taken from the supposed remains of Nicholas II and his family. Genetic fingerprinting methods prove that the remains are genuine.

SUPERMODEL STARS
Supermodels of the fashion industry, such as Cindy Crawford, Christy Turlington, and Linda Evangelista, become stars, known internationally in their own right.

REICHSTAG
In probably the most important artistic aspect of German reunification, Alex Schultes wins the architectural competition to design the administrative district around the Reichstag.

PIANO WINS PALME D'OR
New Zealand film director Jane Campion (b. 1954) becomes the first woman to win the prestigious Palme d'Or at Cannes for her latest film *The Piano*. The film stars Holly Hunter (b. 1958), who also gets an award for her portrayal of the mute heroine who finds expression through her piano playing.

ABOVE: Former President George Bush with Russian premier Boris Yeltsin, who has just survived an attempted coup.

ERITREA INDEPENDENT
The former Italian colony of Eritrea, which has been joined to Ethiopia since 1952, wins its independence. This is in reward for its role in overthrowing the Mengistu government.

ABORIGINAL LAND RIGHTS
In Australia, the federal parliament passes the Native Title Act, recognizing Aboriginal rights to make claims on land taken away from them by early European settlers. The Act follows years of campaigning by Aboriginal rights groups.

FIRST WALK ACROSS ANTARCTICA
English explorer Ranulph Fiennes (b. 1945) and Mike Stroud become the first people to cross Antarctica on foot. After 95 days they are picked up 350 miles from the sea, having walked 1,347 miles pulling sleds loaded with supplies.

HOUSE
British sculptor Rachel Whiteread (b. 1963) inspires controversy with her sculpture *House*. It is a cast of a house in London's East End, made by pouring in concrete and then removing the walls and roof. Whiteread's work is shown in Paris, Chicago, and Berlin.

MANDELA FOR PRESIDENT

South Africa holds multiracial elections and Mandela becomes the country's first black president. Violence breaks out in Rwanda. The IRA announces a cease-fire in Northern Ireland. Russian forces invade breakaway Chechnya. Dead animals pickled in formaldehyde are a talking point in the art world and the long-awaited Channel Tunnel is opened. Fossil remains in Ethiopia help to date human prehistory.

OPPOSITE: Displaced persons, internal refugees in Rwanda, seek safety in Kibeho Camp.

1994

Jan	**31**	The Buffalo Bills lose in the Super Bowl again for a record fourth consecutive time
Feb	**5**	Serb mortar bomb hits a crowded market place in Sarajevo
	23	Cease-fire between Serbia and Croatia in Bosnia
Apr	**6**	The presidents of Burundi and Rwanda are killed in a plane crash; mass violence erupts in Rwanda
	26	First multiracial elections begin in South Africa, resulting in victory for the African National Congress (ANC)
	28	CIA spy Aldrich Ames was sentenced to life in prison on charges of spying for the KGB

May	**1**	Brazilian racing champion Ayrton Senna is killed
	6	Channel Tunnel opens
	10	Nelson Mandela is sworn in as the first black president of South Africa
	19	Jacqueline Kennedy Onassis dies of cancer at the age of 64
Aug	**14**	"Carlos the Jackal," the most wanted terrorist in the world, is arrested
	31	Irish Republican Army (IRA) declares a cease-fire in Northern Ireland
Sep	**19**	U.S. troops invade Haiti
Dec	**11**	Russian forces invade Chechnya following its declaration of independence

ABOVE: *Away from the Flock*, Damien Hirst's contribution to "Sensation," the exhibition of work by young British artists.

PRESIDENT MANDELA

Nelson Mandela becomes the first black president of South Africa following the victory of the African National Congress (ANC) in the country's first multiracial democratic elections.

MASS SLAUGHTER IN RWANDA

Genocide breaks out in Rwanda as the Hutu dominated army and Hutu extremists massacre 500,000 people from the Tutsi majority. The Tutsis establish control and two million Hutus flee for their lives into neighboring Zaire. The genocide and mass exodus follow the death in a plane crash of the presidents of both Rwanda and neighboring Burundi, which experience similar massacres.

NORTHERN IRELAND CEASE-FIRE

Following the Anglo–Irish Downing Street Declaration between the prime ministers of Britain and Ireland, John Major (b. 1943) and Albert Reynolds (b. 1932) to bring peace to Northern Ireland, the Irish Republican Army (IRA) declares a cease-fire. This allows Sinn Fein, their political representatives, to take part in the peace talks.

CHANNEL TUNNEL OPENS

The Channel Tunnel is open. Running under the sea between England and France, it provides a high-speed rail link.

RIGHT: The huge ozone hole over the Antarctic, mapped by the Russian *Meteor 3* satellite.

RUSSIANS INVADE CHECHNYA

Russian troops occupy the rebel Caucasian province of Chechnya after it unilaterally declared independence from Russia. The capital, Grozny, is leveled to the ground in the fighting which continues until an agreement is reached which effectively grants the province de facto independence. The final Russian troops withdraw in January 1997. In May 1997, Russia and Chechnya sign a peace agreement formally ending the separatist war.

YEMEN CIVIL WAR

Tension, which has existed between the Northern and Southern Yemen elites since last year, explodes into war. This follows sporadic clashes when the southern leadership declares secession, as formal unification had taken place in 1990. The fighting involves armor and artillery and in July the Northern forces capture Aden, which had been bombarded with SCUD missiles. In a frenzy of religious zeal, the northerners destroyed the only brewery in the Arabian peninsula.

FINNISH DIAMONDS

Diamond deposits are discovered in northern Finland, leading to hopes that there are very large deposits in the region.

PEACE IN COLOMBIA

In Colombia, the government reaches peace with four left-wing guerrilla groups.

SARAJEVO BOMBED

In February, a Serb 120mm mortar bomb hits a crowded market place in Sarajevo, killing 68 people and seriously wounding 200 more. Subsequently, Serb forces bombard safe areas in Goradze and Srebrenica. NATO authorizes air strikes on Serbian posts, galvanizing the Contact Group of United States, Britain, Russia, and Germany.

AWAY FROM THE FLOCK SHOCKS

British artist Damien Hirst (b. 1965) provokes controversy and debate in the media with his work. This year sees *Away from the Flock*, featuring a dead lamb preserved in a glass tank of formaldehyde. Last year he used a similar technique to display *Mother and Child Divided*, a cow and calf sliced in half.

U.S. INTO HAITI

The U.S. Army lands on the island of Haiti to restore civilian rule after a military coup deposed Jean-Bertrand Aristide, the democratically elected president, in September 1991. Presidential elections held in August 1995 result in victory for René Préval, a close associate of Aristide.

PULP FICTION

American director Quentin Tarantino (b. 1963) of *Reservoir Dogs* fame produces a new film titled *Pulp Fiction*. It stars John Travolta and Harvey Keitel, and is inspired by thrillers of the 1950s and 1960s.

KANSAI AIRPORT

Japan's new airport, one of the largest civil engineering projects of recent years, has opened. The buildings are designed by Renzo Piano and are sited on a specially created artificial island.

COMET HITS JUPITER

Chunks of Comet Shoemaker-Levy 9 collide with the planet Jupiter in July, producing fiery plumes of gas; the comet had broken up in Jupiter's magnetic field.

MISSING LINK

The uncertainty surrounding human origins becomes a little clearer when anthropologists announce the discovery in Ethiopia of fossils of *Australopithecus ramidus*, the earliest direct ancestors of humans. The fossils are 4.4 million years old.

MASS SUICIDE

Members of an international religious cult, Order of the Solar Temple, commit mass suicide in Switzerland and Canada. It is one of a number of mass suicides and other events by members of religious cults heralding the end of the millennium.

ABOVE: Brazilian racing champion Ayrton Senna is killed when his car crashes in the Grand Prix race at Monza, Italy.

EUTHANASIA PERMITTED

Oregon voters support Measure 16 permitting euthanasia in regulated circumstances.

WINTER OLYMPICS

The 17th Winter Olympics take place in the Norwegian town of Lillehammer just two years after the previous Winter Games. Television revenues are the reason for splitting the winter and summer games.

BUFFALO LOSES AGAIN

The Buffalo Bills establish a new Super Bowl record of futility when they appear in their fourth consecutive Super Bowl and lose to the Dallas Cowboys 30-13.

BRAZIL WINS WORLD CUP

Brazil wins a record fourth soccer World Cup. The controversial decision to stage the World Cup in the United States, not a soccer power, is a success and leads to the formation of Major League Soccer in the U.S.

AYRTON SENNA
(1960–1994)

Brazilian motor racing legend Ayrton Senna has died after a 190 mph crash in the San Marino Grand Prix at Monza in Italy. In his tragically short career, he won 41 Grand Prix races and was three times Formula One world racing champion, in 1988, 1990, and 1992.

PEACE IN BOSNIA

The Dayton Peace Accord ends three years of fighting in Bosnia. A terrorist bomb explodes in Oklahoma. Israeli prime minister Yitzhak Rabin is assassinated. Worldwide outrage follows renewed nuclear testing and the execution of writer and human rights campaigner Ken Saro-Wiwa. An earthquake devastates the port of Kobe, Japan. Astronomers discover a brown dwarf and a talking pig becomes an unlikely film star.

OPPOSITE: The U.S. space shuttle *Atlantis* photographed from the Russian *Mir* space station.

1995

Jan	6	Tamils sign cease-fire in Sri Lanka but fighting resumes
	17	Earthquake devastates Kobe, Japan
Mar	20	Turkish forces launch an attack against the Kurds
Apr	19	Federal Building is bombed in Oklahoma City
July	11	Serbs capture a U.N. designated safe area of Srebrenica, Bosnia
	20	Serbs attack a U.N. safe haven in Bihac, Bosnia
Aug	4	Croatian forces invade the Serb inhabited region of Krajina, Croatia
	30	NATO begins attacks on Serb positions in Bosnia
Nov	21	Peace accord signed in Dayton, Ohio between Bosnia, Serbia, and Croatia
Nov	4	Israeli prime minister Yitzhak Rabin is assassinated
	11	Nigerian writer and human rights campaigner Ken Saro-Wiwa executed
Dec	28	International protests following French nuclear tests

ABOVE: Yitzhak Rabin is assassinated in Tel Aviv.

BOSNIAN CRISIS

In July, the Serbs overrun the U.N. protected zones of Srebrenica and massacre the male population. They also besiege Bihac. The following month Serbs bombard Sarajevo, killing 37 people and leading NATO to attack infrastructure targets in Serb-held Bosnia. Following pressure on the Bosnian Serb leader Radovan Karadzic by President Milosevic of Serbia, heavy weapons are withdrawn from around Sarajevo. In November, at Dayton, Ohio, a peace agreement is signed, bringing an end to the Bosnian conflict. It splits the state 51-49 between the Bosnian and Croat Federation and the Republika Srpska (Bosnian Serbs). The settlement creates a unified Bosnia but in fact divides the country into two self-governing parts, a Muslim-Croat federation and a Bosnian-Serb republic.

ABOVE: Ruins of the Alfred Murrah Federal Building in Oklahoma City after a bomb has destroyed it. Timothy McVeigh will later be charged with planting the bomb.

LEFT: Filmmaker and comic Woody Allen directs *Mighty Aphrodite*, a comedy about love, marriage, and adopted children. At this time he is receiving bad press about his relationship with his adopted daughter.

ABOVE: A Bosnian Serb refugee from Krajina waits patiently in a government center. The plan is to reintegrate refugees into society.

SARO-WIWA EXECUTED
In Nigeria, the dissident writer and human rights campaigner Ken Saro-Wiwa (1941–1995) and eight others are executed by the military government, prompting international outrage. Saro-Wiwa has led the protests by the Ogoni people of southern Nigeria against exploitation of their land by international oil companies. His death causes Nigeria to be suspended from the Commonwealth and sanctions are imposed.

NEW EU MEMBERS
Austria, Sweden, and Finland join the EU, bringing its members up to 13. Many other states, including the Czech Republic, Hungary, Poland, Estonia, Slovenia, and Cyprus are hoping to join.

POWDER HER FACE
British composer Thomas Adès attracts critical praise for his opera *Powder her Face*. It is based on the sometimes scandalous life of Margaret, Duchess of Argyll.

MILKY WAY BLACK HOLE
U.S. astronomers report detecting signs of a black hole in our own galaxy, the Milky Way.

ANTIATOMS
A team of German, Italian, and Swiss physicists make the first antiatoms. They last for only a fraction of a second before colliding with ordinary atoms and vanishing.

ORBITING JUPITER
In December the U.S. spacecraft *Galileo*, launched in 1989, goes into orbit around Jupiter and starts sending pictures and data back to Earth.

KOBE EARTHQUAKE
The Great Hanshin earthquake devastates Kobe in Japan. More than 2,700 lose their lives and over 1,000 buildings are destroyed, as well as the region's roads and power supplies. The earthquake measured 7.2 on the Richter scale and is the worst earthquake to hit Japan since 1923.

ROAD PROTESTERS
In Britain, environmentalists protest against the building of a new road through ancient British woodland. They tunnel into the forest floor and build tree houses to prevent the felling of 10,000 trees. The protesters are evicted but their cause attracts considerable publicity and sympathy.

BANNING LIVE ANIMAL EXPORTS
Animal rights activists achieve a temporary ban on exporting live animals from a British port. They claim that animals are carried in overcrowded conditions and deprived of food and water for long periods. They aim for an EU ban on such practices.

OKLAHOMA CITY BOMBING
Federal government offices in Oklahoma City are blown up in a rare terrorist bombing in the United States. The blast kills 167 people. Two men are later indicted for the crime. Both are associated with militias which are fanatically opposed to the federal government.

SRI LANKA
Despite a temporary cease-fire, fighting resumes between the government and the Tamils. A state of emergency is reintroduced.

FRENCH NUCLEAR TESTING
In defiance of world opinion, France renews underground nuclear testing on Mururoa Atoll in the South Pacific. France carries out a series of tests before ending them in January 1996 and signing the Nuclear Test-Ban Treaty, which it had previously refused to do.

RABIN ASSASSINATED
Prime Minister Yitzhak Rabin is assassinated by a Hebrew fanatic in Tel Aviv, Israel, soon after leaving a peace rally. He is succeeded by Simon Peres. However, Rabin's assassination jeopardizes the peace process with the Palestinians when Peres loses the general election in May 1996 to the right-winger Benyamin Netanyahu (b. 1949), who is opposed to the land for peace deal.

BROWN DWARF DISCOVERED
Astronomers discover a brown dwarf, a strange object smaller than a star but larger than a planet. The existence of brown dwarfs has long been suspected but never proved.

TALIBAN, HUTUS, AND BRITISH BEEF

Taliban seizes Kabul in Afghanistan and imposes strict Islamic law. The Guatemalan civil war ends after 36 years of fighting. Tutsis attack Hutu refugees in Zaire. Prime minister Benazir Bhutto is dismissed from office. U.S. president Bill Clinton is elected for a second term. The EU bans British beef after fears of Mad Cow Disease. A bomb blast mars the centenary Olympic Games.

1996

Feb	17	Space probe NEAR is launched
Mar	13	Sixteen schoolchildren and their teacher are killed by a gunman in Dunblane, Scotland
	25	The European Union bans the export of British beef after fears of Mad Cow Disease
Apr	29	U.N. war crimes tribunal opens in The Hague, Netherlands, to investigate alleged crimes against humanity in the Yugoslav civil war
July	27	Bomb explodes at the Olympic Games in Atlanta during a concert at Centennial Olympic Park killing two
Aug	31	Iraqi aircraft violate U.N. no-fly zone
Sep	3	United States launches cruise missiles against Iraq
Sep	12	Rap star Tupac Shakur dies of gunshot wounds at the age of 25
	17	Former Vice President Spiro Agnew, who resigned from office after taking kickbacks from contractors, dies at the age of 73
	27	Taliban takes control of Kabul, Afghanistan
Oct	21	U.N. reports that 250,000 Hutu refugees have fled Zaire
Nov	5	Bill Clinton is elected U.S. president for his second term
	15	Tutsi rebels defeat extremist Hutu militiamen
Dec	12	Madeleine Albright becomes the first female Secretary of State
	17	Tupac guerrillas seize hostages in Lima, Peru
	29	Civil war ends in Guatemala

ABOVE: A U.S. military engineer directs traffic across the pontoon bridge built to link Croatia and Bosnia-Herzegovina.

BELOW: A U.S. Howitzer at work during Operation Joint Endeavor, part of the response to the crisis in former Yugoslavia.

TALIBAN TAKE KABUL

The Islamic fundamentalist Taliban militia take control of Afghanistan's capital, Kabul, imposing strict Islamic law and forcing women to wear a full veil in public and all men to grow beards. Their control of the country is far from complete, but Taliban brings a measure of peace to Afghanistan not enjoyed since the Russian invasion in 1979.

RWANDAN REFUGEES

More than one million Hutu refugees from Rwanda living in refugee camps are attacked by Tutsis supported by the Rwandan government, driving them from their camps. Many die from cholera and other diseases, causing a major humanitarian crisis in Zaire and destabilizing the government of President Mobutu (b. 1930). During November, 400,000 of the Hutus return home to Rwanda after the extremists responsible for the 1994 genocide in Rwanda are driven out of the refugee camps.

BENAZIR BHUTTO DISMISSED

In Pakistan, Prime Minister Benazir Bhutto (b. 1953) is dismissed by the president for corruption for the second time in her career. Bhutto was the daughter of former prime minister Zulfikar Ali Bhutto, who was overthrown and then executed by the military in 1978. She first became prime minister in 1988 after the fall of the military government, but was dismissed in 1990. She won reelection in 1993 but persistent charges of corruption against her, and in particular her husband, remove her from power once again.

ABOVE: Animal rights activists demonstrate in London as BSE is discovered in cattle and is feared to affect human beings.

CLINTON WINS SECOND TERM

U.S. president Bill Clinton wins a second term in office against Republican Bob Dole, taking 49 percent of the popular vote against 41 percent for Dole. Democrats fail to win Congress and face problems getting legislation through against Republican opposition.

KURDS CAPTURE SULAIMANIYA

The Kurdish Democratic Party (KDP), fighting with Iraqi assistance, captures the city of Sulaimaniya. It is the stronghold of the umbrella anti-Iraqi organization the Patriotic Union of Kurdistan (PUK). The KDP bomb a Kurdish refugee camp in Iran. Sulaimaniya is recaptured in October.

TUPAC GUERRILLAS SEIZE HOSTAGES

Movimiento Revolucionario Tupac Amaru (MRTA) guerrillas seize 460 hostages at the Japanese ambassador's residence in Lima, Peru. All but 72 hostages are released through negotiations. In April 1997, Peruvian special forces storm the residence, kill the 14 members of MRTA, then release the hostages.

HUGE DINOSAUR

Fossil bones of a huge carnivorous dinosaur are found in the Sahara. The dinosaur is larger than the famous *Tyrannosaurus rex*, but similar to another dinosaur found in South America eight months earlier.

PEACE IN GUATEMALA

Left-wing guerrillas in Guatemala sign a peace agreement with the government and end 36 years of civil war. Two years later, the Roman Catholic Church reports that the civil war has caused the deaths of 150,000 members of the rural Native American majority with a further 50,000 listed as missing.

TOP: An Italian soldier clearing land mines at Praca in Bosnia. When the fighting is over, the mines present a danger to civilians.

ABOVE: A U.S. soldier mans an IFOR (International Force) checkpoint on the road that leads to Tuzla, Bosnia-Herzegovina.

TRAINSPOTTING

The film *Trainspotting* is premiered. Starring Robert Carlyle, the film is based on a novel by Irving Welsh and takes a sometimes funny, sometimes brutal look at the Scottish drug scene.

TOY STORY

A new film, *Toy Story*, opens. It features the adventures of a group of toys and is the first full-length feature film to be made completely by computer animation.

ASTEROID PROBE

Space probe NEAR (Near Earth Asteroid Rendezvous) is launched on February 17 to investigate the asteroid Eros, a rugged 25 mile long lump of rock between Mars and Jupiter.

MAD COW DISEASE

British scientists report a new variant of a rare fatal illness of the human nervous system, Creutzfeldt-Jakob Disease (CJD). It is linked to eating beef from cattle infected with bovine spongiform encephalopathy (BSE), or mad cow disease. BSE was identified in 1986 in cows fed with animal protein from sheep infected with a nervous disease, scrapie. In March, the EU bans the export of British beef.

SUBMARINE SUICIDES

North Korean infiltrators commit suicide when their Sang-O-class submarine with 26 men on board runs aground off South Korea in September. Thirteen were killed by South Korean forces, while ten appear to have been executed by an officer who, rather than be captured, committed suicide.

CENTENARY OLYMPICS

The 100th Olympic Games are held in Atlanta. Eleven thousand athletes from 197 nations attend. Kerri Strug's brave vault with an injured ankle helps the American women's team to gold in gymnastics, while Canadian Donovan Bailey claims gold and a world record time of 9.84 seconds in the 100m. The biggest star of the track events is Michael Johnson of the United States. He wins two golds with victories in the 200m and 400m, winning the 200m in the fastest time ever. Michelle Smith takes three swimming golds and a bronze back home to Ireland. Sport, however, is again obscured by violence when a bomb explodes in Olympic Park, killing two and injuring 11.

TINY MOTORS

U.S. engineers announce the construction of micromotors about 1mm (.039 inches) square, which can drive gears thinner than a human hair.

LEFT: Refugees from Zaire shelter in Nyaragusu Camp, Kigoma, Tanzania. Diseases such as cholera are a problem in the camps.

BELOW: Zairean refugees flee the fighting in their country, cramming into small boats to cross Lake Tanganyika to Tanzania.

DEATH OF A PRINCESS

Diana, Princess of Wales, dies suddenly in a car crash in Paris. Financial crisis hits Southeast Asia when the value of the Thai baht collapses. Socialists and Social Democrats dominate European elections. Hong Kong reverts to Chinese control. Scientists successfully clone a sheep for the first time. The world watches three-tailed comet Hale-Bopp as it passes the Earth, and girl power hits the charts.

OPPOSITE: Thousands leave flowers at the gates of Kensington Palace, London, in honor of a dead princess.

1997

Jan	20	President Clinton is sworn in for his second term in office
	26	Violence occurs in Albania after the collapse of pyramid saving schemes
Feb	4	O.J. Simpson is found guilty in a civil court for the wrongful death of his ex-wife Nicole Brown and friend Ron Goldman
	27	Announcement is made that British geneticists have cloned a sheep
Apr	22	Peruvian special forces storm the occupied Japanese embassy in Lima, killing 14 Tupac guerrillas and releasing their hostages
May	1	Labour Party wins the British general election
	12	Russia and Chechnya sign a peace agreement
May	29	Tutsi rebels take Kinshasa, Zaire. They rename the country the Democratic Republic of Congo
June	1	Socialist Party wins the general election in France
	2	Timothy McVeigh is found guilty of the Oklahoma City bombing
July	1	Hong Kong reverts to Chinese control
	2	Economic crisis begins in Southeast Asia
Aug	31	Diana, Princess of Wales, is killed in a car crash. Dodi Fayed, her escort, also dies in the accident
Sept	7	Former President of Zaire, Mobutu, dies of cancer just months after fleeing his country

ABOVE: The Spice Girls, living embodiment of "girl power" at the premiere of their film *Spice, the Movie*.

EUROPEAN ELECTIONS

In Britain, Tony Blair (b. 1953) leads the Labour Party to a landslide victory after 18 years of Conservative government. Victories for the French Socialists in June and the German Social Democrats in September 1998 removing Helmut Kohl after 16 years in power, lead to Socialist or Social Democratic governments in almost every Western European nation.

HONG KONG

A British crown colony since 1841, Hong Kong reverts to Chinese rule. The Chinese agree to respect existing laws and economic structures, although democratic institutions are swiftly replaced by an assembly appointed by Beijing.

MOTHER TERESA OF CALCUTTA (born AGNES GONXHA BOJAXHIU) (1910–1997)

The Yugoslav-born Roman Catholic missionary Mother Teresa, whose work in Calcutta is known throughout the world, has died. In 1928, Mother Teresa joined the Sisters of Loretto in Calcutta and taught in their convent until 1948 when she left to work alone with the poor. In 1950 she founded her sisterhood, the Order of the Missionaries of Charity, which now has some 2,000 sisters caring for the poor and sick.

DEATH OF DIANA

Diana, Princess of Wales, is killed in a car crash in Paris. Her death causes an international outpouring of grief and leads to a sharp fall in the popularity of the British monarchy, whom many consider treated her poorly during her life. An estimated two billion people worldwide watch the funeral service on television. Her campaign to rid the world of land mines is successful in 1998 when an international treaty forbidding their use is signed in Ottawa.

FINANCIAL COLLAPSE

The collapse in value of the Thai baht leads to a financial crisis throughout Southeast Asia as banks collapse and currencies lose their value. The crisis, caused by excessive national debt and poor financial controls, spreads to Japan, Indonesia, and Russia, and then in 1999 to Brazil. Although the International Monetary Fund launches a rescue package for affected countries, the economic downturn creates chaos throughout the world's markets and leads to fears of a recession to match that of the 1930s.

MOBUTU DEFEATED

President Mobutu, leader and dictator of Zaire since 1965, loses power after rebels led by Laurent Kabilia overthrow his government. As leader, Mobutu treated Zaire as his personal bank account, bleeding the country dry and causing economic ruin.

FINANCIAL COLLAPSE IN ALBANIA

The small eastern European country of Albania descends into anarchy after the collapse of corrupt pyramid investment schemes. Albanians who have lost all their savings take to the streets, looting weapons from the army and attacking the government. Foreign nationals are evacuated and the government calls for elections, which result in a landslide victory for the opposition Socialist Party in June.

BRITISH AND RUSSIAN AGREEMENT

In March, the British and Russian governments sign an agreement on joint military training and information exchange on new weapons.

SPICE POWER

Girl power in the form of the Spice Girls, Posh, Baby, Sporty, Scary, and Ginger, is the latest success in the world of pop. The all-girl British band is achieving worldwide success with a string of bestselling numbers.

E. COLI MAPPED

An American team of geneticists led by Fred Blattner compile the complete genetic code of the bacterium *Escherichia coli*, which contains more than 4,200 genes. Some forms of *E. coli* cause food poisoning; this year an outbreak of *E. coli* bacteria derived from eating contaminated meat occurs in the U.K.

ABOVE: Dolly the sheep, the world's first adult animal clone, with Dr. Ron James, head of PPL Therapeutics at Edinburgh's Roslin Institute.

ABOVE: Sarajevo, the Serbian capital, begins to rebuild as peace settles in the troubled countries of the former Yugoslavia.

THE FULL MONTY

A new British film is gaining unexpected success internationally. Directed by Peter Cattaneo, *The Full Monty* features a group of unemployed men in the north of England who turn to stripping to earn a living. It extracts hilarious comedy from social deprivation.

DOLLY THE SHEEP

Scottish scientists announce that they have cloned a sheep from a cell taken from an adult animal; the sheep is nicknamed Dolly. This is the first successful cloning using nonreproductive cells. DNA from an adult cell was combined with an unfertilized egg that had had its DNA removed.

HALE-BOPP

Comet Hale-Bopp, a comet with three tails, nears the Sun in April. A mass of rock, dust, and ice, the comet is named after the two American astronomers who first saw it: Alan Hale and Thomas Bopp. The comet will not return for 2,400 years.

CULT SUICIDE

As Comet Hale-Bopp appears, the brightest comet visible for 400 years, 39 members of the Heaven's Gate cult in San Diego commit mass suicide. The cult's members believed that they were to escape Earth's destruction by rendezvousing with a space vehicle that was to be hidden behind the comet.

GUGGENHEIM MUSEUM

One of the most striking of recent buildings is the Guggenheim Museum in Bilbao. Designed by Frank O. Gehry, the building has a striking metal clad facade in which curved forms seem to invite the visitor into a mysterious space.

FLOODS CAUSE HOMELESSNESS

Flash floods make 70,000 homeless in the Czech Republic, Germany, and Poland.

TIGER WOODS

U.S. golfer Eldrick "Tiger" Woods wins the Masters golf tournament at Augusta at age 21, by a 12 stroke victory.

MCDONALD'S CLEARED

The longest trial in English history ends when fast food chain McDonald's is cleared of damaging the environment. McDonald's sued two protesters, David Morris and Helen Steel, for distributing leaflets criticizing the American chain's environmental record.

OFF TO SATURN

The spacecraft *Cassini/Huygens* is launched on a voyage to Saturn and scheduled to arrive in 2004.

DIANA, PRINCESS OF WALES
(1961–1997)

The world is shocked by the sudden and violent death of Diana, Princess of Wales, who has been killed in Paris during a car chase involving the press. The former wife of HRH the Prince of Wales (they divorced in 1996), she had been a constant focus of media attention since taking on her public role. She was actively involved in the work of many charities, but since 1994 had been working principally for the International Red Cross. Recently, she had spearheaded the campaign against land mines. She was in the company of Dodi Fayed when she was killed.

SEX, TRUTH, AND RECONCILIATION

In the United States, President Clinton avoids impeachment following an investigation into his alleged affair. In South Africa, the Truth and Reconciliation Committee publishes its report. Tension rises again in Serbia. Former Chilean dictator Pinochet is arrested. Terrorists bomb U.S. embassies in Kenya and Tanzania. The Good Friday Peace Agreement brings peace to Northern Ireland. A hurricane devastates Central America. Viagra is the new wonder drug for impotence.

OPPOSITE: Bill Clinton, seen here with his wife and daughter, has a troubled year in office.

1998

Jan	21	Investigation is launched into President Clinton's alleged affair with a White House intern
Mar	5	NASA scientists announce evidence of water on the Moon
Apr	10	Good Friday Peace Agreement brings peace settlement for Northern Ireland
May	6	Mudslides devastate towns in Italy
	20	Indonesian president Suharto resigns following riots
	28	Pakistan explodes five nuclear devices
Aug	7	Terrorists bomb U.S. embassies in Nairobi, Kenya and Dar-es-Salaam, Tanzania
Sept	24	Iran lifts fatwa on author Salman Rushdie
Oct	12	NATO threatens an air strike against Serbia
	18	International observers arrive in the Serbian province of Kosovo
	18	Former Chilean dictator General Augusto Pinochet is arrested in London
	24	Troops from South Africa and Botswana enter Lesotho
	29	Truth and Reconciliation Committee publishes report in South Africa
Dec	16	American and British air strikes are launched against Iraq

ABOVE: Frank Sinatra, "Ol' Blue Eyes," dies this year.

CLINTON SEX SCANDAL

President Clinton is accused of having an affair with a White House intern and asking her to lie about it. The allegations are investigated by an independent prosecutor, Kenneth Starr, and eventually lead to an attempt by the U.S. Congress to impeach the president for perjury and other offenses in November. The president gives evidence on television to the House of Representatives, but despite pressure from Republicans, Clinton is not removed from office.

GOOD FRIDAY AGREEMENT

In Northern Ireland, political parties from Unionist and Nationalist communities sign the Good Friday Peace Agreement setting up an elected assembly and new institutions linking the North with the Republic. The agreement, which is overseen by Northern Ireland Secretary Mo Mowlam (b. 1949), also sets up a process to encourage paramilitary groups to decommission their weapons. The Unionist leader, David Trimble, and the Nationalist John Hume jointly receive the 1998 Nobel Peace Prize for their work in securing the agreement.

TITANIC

Starring Leonardo di Caprio and Kate Winslett, the disaster movie *Titanic* is the most expensive film ever made and a smash hit, taking 11 Academy Awards.

SUHARTO RESIGNS

In Indonesia, following economic collapse, demonstrators force the resignation of President Suharto, leader since 1967. He is succeeded by his deputy, Jusuf Habibie, who promises to end corruption and nepotism in government.

U.S. EMBASSIES BOMBED

Islamic fundamentalists bomb the U.S. embassies in Nairobi, Kenya, and Dar-es-Salaam, Tanzania, killing 257 people and injuring hundreds more. In retaliation, U.S. warships launch Tomahawk cruise missiles at targets in Afghanistan and Sudan in an attempt to kill Osama bin Laden, the Saudi millionaire who has been identified with terrorist bombings against U.S. targets in Africa and the Middle East. The cruise missile attack does not kill him. Also, U.S. intelligence incorrectly identified a pharmaceuticals factory in Khartoum, Sudan, as a chemical warfare factory.

KOSOVO

International observers are sent to the Serbian province of Kosovo to police a cease-fire agreed between Kosovan freedom fighters and the Serbian army after NATO threatens air strikes against Serbia. The province, which is almost entirely Albanian in population, is fighting for independence from Serbia, which suspended the provincial constitution in March 1991 and introduced repressive measures against the Albanian population. The war is the latest chapter in the disintegration of the former Yugoslavia which began in 1991.

TRUTH AND RECONCILIATION

The report of the Truth and Reconciliation Commission, chaired by Nobel Peace Prize winner Archbishop Desmond Tutu, is published. The Commission took evidence from many people in an attempt to reconcile the differences left by apartheid. The report condemns apartheid as a crime against humanity but finds the ruling African National Congress (ANC) as well as white-only parties to have been guilty of human rights violations.

PINOCHET ARRESTED

Former Chilean dictator Augusto Pinochet is arrested in London after Spanish judges apply for his extradition to Spain to face charges of murder and torture. Following legal debates over whether Pinochet has legal immunity in 1999, the High Court decides that he does not. The British Home Secretary Jack Straw (b. 1946) orders his extradition.

LESOTHO

The Pretoria government in South Africa sends troops into Lesotho to restore calm following civil unrest.

OPERATION DESERT FOX

The United States and Britain carry out air strikes against Iraqi targets following Saddam Hussein's noncompliance with U.N. weapons inspectors. The U.S. Navy, U.S. Air Force, and RAF launch 650 attacks. The U.S. Navy launches 325 Tomahawk cruise missiles and the U.S.A.F. B-52s launch 90 cruise missiles against 100 targets including Republican Guard barracks and chemical and biological warfare installations in Iraq.

BIRTHDAY LETTERS

Britain's Poet Laureate Ted Hughes (1930–1998) publishes poems he has written about the suicide of his first wife, American poet Sylvia Plath. The book, which appears just before Hughes's death, wins critical acclaim and sells in large numbers.

NUCLEAR TESTING

India joins the nuclear club by testing nuclear devices in Rajasthan. Pakistan retaliates by testing five devices, although both pledge to sign the Nuclear Test Ban Treaty at some stage.

FAST SELLING VIAGRA

Viagra, a new treatment for impotence, has become the fastest selling prescription drug.

ITALIAN EARTHQUAKE

Frescoes by Italian artist Giotto are destroyed after an earthquake in Assisi. There is controversy over whether the works of art could have been better protected.

CODE COMPLETED

For the first time, scientists compile the complete code of an invertebrate animal, a tiny worm.

FLYING GALAXIES

Astronomers discover that the galaxies in space are flying apart at ever increasing speeds against the force of gravity.

CIRCADIAN CLOCK

Research shows that nearly all living organisms, not just people, have a built-in mechanism, the "circadian clock." It uses light and temperature to keep track of night and day.

WINTER OLYMPICS

The Winter Olympics in Nagano, Japan are a resounding success in front of huge crowds. The speed skating record book is rewritten with the use of the clap skate, invented in Holland. The new skates, named for the noise they make, have a spring-loaded hinge at the front which allows the racer's heel to rise without lifting the blade of the skate from the ice. Dutch skaters win five golds and six other medals and five world records are broken. The Czech Republic scores a shocking victory in ice hockey by beating the NHL professionals of Canada and America, while American Tara Lipinski captures figure skating gold.

FRANCE WINS WORLD CUP

France wins the football World Cup in Paris. The defeat of Brazil in the final was surrounded by intrigue over the poor performance of Brazilian star Ronaldo.

DRUGS DOMINATE TOUR DE FRANCE

The Tour de France is disrupted by revelations of drug use by cyclists and team support for the abuse. The discovery of a team masseur carrying banned drugs leads to a police investigation, arrests, and then protests by racers, who complain of victimization. Cycling's top event is completed but the sport's image is tarnished.

BASEBALL

Mark McGwire, the first-baseman for the St. Louis Cardinals, hits his 62nd home run of the season to pass Roger Maris's record. His race with Sammy Sosa of the Chicago Cubs to reach the record delights baseball fans. McGwire finishes with 70 homers, Sosa with 66.

POL POT DEAD

The body of the former leader of the Khmer Rouge, Pol Pot, has been put on display in northern Cambodia. Due for trial, he may have committed suicide or have been murdered. During his rule over Cambodia (1975–1979) he was responsible for some 1.7 million deaths.

DEVASTATING HURRICANE

Hurricane Mitch causes devastation in Honduras, Nicaragua, El Salvador, and Guatemala before heading across Mexico into the Caribbean. More than 10,000 people are killed and whole towns are swept away.

BELOW: The "Agreement," the document produced as a result of the Northern Ireland peace talks, is torn up by a Unionist supporter.

NATO BOMBS AND KOSOVAN REFUGEES

War breaks out in the Balkans when NATO begins air strikes against the Serbian military targets in Yugoslavia. The action intensifies Serbian "cleansing" of ethnic Albanians and thousands flee Kosovo. The single European currency is introduced and the EU Commission resigns after evidence of fraud. King Hussein of Jordan dies. Lockerbie suspects are brought to trial. New research suggests flirting is good for you.

OPPOSITE: Nelson Mandela bows out of South African politics.

1999

Jan	1	European single currency begins
	24	Cash for votes scandal hits the International Olympic Committee (IOC); six members resign
	26	U.S. missile hits a residential area in Basra, Iraq
Feb	7	King Hussein of Jordan dies at age 64
	12	President Clinton is acquitted of perjury and obstruction of justice
	15	Abdullah Ocalan, leader of the Kurdish Workers Party (PKK), is captured in Nairobi by Turkish special forces
	23	Britain completes the destruction of its stocks of antipersonnel mines
Mar	7	United States threatens trade war against Europe for importing bananas from former U.S. colonies in the Caribbean and Africa
Mar	15	All members of the European Commission resign over a report of fraud
	24	NATO begins air strikes against Serbia
	31	Serb forces capture three U.S. soldiers
Apr	5	Two Libyans suspected of the Lockerbie bombing arrive in Netherlands for trial
May	17	Ehud Barak is elected prime minister of Israel in a landslide victory
July	16	John F. Kennedy, Jr. is killed piloting his own plane
Aug	17	Devastating earthquake hits Turkey and measures 7.4 on the Richter scale

NEW NATO MEMBERS

Hungary, Poland, and the Czech Republic join NATO, the first former Communist countries in Eastern Europe to do so. All three countries are also applying to join the EU.

SINGLE EUROPEAN CURRENCY

The European single currency begins in 11 EU nations, including France and Germany but not Britain. The Euro, which can only be used in paper transactions, will initially run alongside the different national currencies. It will replace them in 2002, when the national currencies will be abolished and Euro notes and coins will circulate freely.

FRAUD IN EU

All 20 members of the EU Commission resign following a report into alleged fraud, which finds the executive guilty of mismanagement, corruption, and nepotism. Former Italian prime minister Romano Prodi is appointed new president of the commission.

NATO BOMBS YUGOSLAVIA

In March, aircraft and cruise missiles from 12 NATO nations launch air attacks against more than 40 targets in Yugoslavia after Serbia refuses to agree to peace negotiations over Kosovo. Serb troops in Kosovo force ethnic Kosovan Albanians across neighboring borders. By the end of March some 300,000 have been displaced. Three U.S. soldiers from the 1st Infantry Division are captured at Kumanovo, Macedonia by Serb forces who have crossed the border. U.S. politician Jesse Jackson later negotiates their release.

INSTITUTIONAL RACISM

In Britain, the inquiry into the murder of a black teenager, Stephen Lawrence, finds that the police had mishandled the case and are guilty of institutional racism. In the United States, a white supremacist is convicted of murdering a black man, James Byrd, in Texas.

BERLIN IS GERMANY'S CAPITAL

For the first time since the war, Berlin becomes the capital of Germany again as the government moves back from Bonn. Since the fall of the Berlin Wall in 1990 and the reunification of Germany, Berlin has been extensively rebuilt to accommodate the new government buildings.

CIVIL WAR IN SIERRA LEONE

Fighting intensifies in Sierra Leone when forces of the Revolutionary United Front (RUF) loot and burn Freetown. President Kabbah has criticized Liberia for supporting the rebels. Civil war began in 1991. In 1996, Ahmed Kabbah was democratically elected president but was overthrown nine months later by the RUF. In 1997, backed by 5,000 men from the Nigerian backed ECOMOG force, he returned to power, but the RUF has continued fighting.

KURDISH LEADER CAPTURED

Turkish special forces in Nairobi capture the Kurdish leader Abdullah Ocalan. The capture precipitates protests throughout Europe as Kurds blame Greek diplomats for allowing their leader to be captured.

NEW ISRAELI PRIME MINISTER

Labor leader and Israel's most decorated soldier, Ehud Barak, is elected Israel's new prime minister, defeating right-winger Binyamin Netanyahu in a landslide victory. Barak's election will pave the way for a fresh start to Middle East peace talks.

SISTINE CHAPEL CEILING

The cleaning of Michelangelo's famous painted ceiling in the Vatican's Sistine Chapel is completed. It shows the familiar paintings in an unfamiliar light, much brighter in color. Experts are divided over the result, some saying that the cleaning has brought the ceiling as close as possible to its original condition, others saying that the work has been too radical.

MIRROR FAILURE

A Russian attempt to create an artificial "moon" to light up dark areas of the country fails when a space mirror fails to unfurl from space station *Mir*.

STARDUST TRIP

Space probe *Stardust* sets off on a 3 billion mile journey to rendezvous with Comet Wild-2, carrying instruments to collect dust from the comet in order to learn more about it.

EXTRATERRESTRIAL CHAIR

The first academic chair for an astronomer to search for extraterrestrial intelligence is founded at the University of California at Berkeley; first professor is William Welch.

GENETICALLY MODIFIED FOODS DEBATE

In the U.K., the safety of genetically modified foods comes under intense debate. Various pressure groups and some scientists demand that the British government impose a moratorium on developing new GM crops.

FLIRTING IS GOOD FOR YOU

Research published in *Psychology Today* suggests that flirting may be designed to ensure that we attract the right mate. According to some research, flirting, far from being superficial behavior, may be a deeply ingrained means of exchanging vital information about the health and reproductive fitness of a potential partner.

THE WHOLE WOMAN

Australian feminist Germaine Greer publishes *The Whole Woman*, a sequel to *The Female Eunuch*, one of the landmark books of the Women's Liberation Movement. In her new book, Greer states that feminism has lost its way and women need to get angry again.

MICHAEL JORDAN RETIRES — AGAIN

Michael Jordan, on whose back professional basketball rose to international prominence, announces his second retirement. Jordan led the Chicago Bulls to six NBA titles; three before his first retirement and three after.

LOCKERBIE SUSPECTS

In April, the two Libyan intelligence officers believed to be responsible for the Lockerbie explosion in 1988 are flown to an air force base in Holland to be tried under Scottish law.

BANANA WAR

The United States threatens a trade war with Europe claiming that Europe favors bananas imported from former U.S. colonies in the Caribbean and Africa. Caribbean producing countries St. Lucia and Dominica threaten to stall World Trade Organization talks.

KING HUSSEIN
(IBN TALAL) OF JORDAN
(1935–1999)

King Hussein of Jordan has died after a battle with cancer. Educated at Harrow and Sandhurst in England, he had ruled Jordan for 46 years and is widely accredited as an influential peacemaker in the troubled Middle East. More than 50 foreign leaders and 800,000 Jordanians gathered for his funeral.

ABOVE: A family of Kosovan Albanians flee Serbian torture and executions.

BELOW: A distressed young Albanian demonstrates the misery of conflict.

WAR CRIME INDICTMENT

As diplomats work to reduce differences between the West and Russia over plans to end the Kosovo crisis, the International War Crimes Tribunal announces that it plans to indict Serb leader Slobodan Milosevic, therefore reducing his incentive to compromise. At the same time, NATO announces that it will increase the number of troops on standby in neighboring Macedonia to 50,000. By June, Serbia announces agreement to a peace deal proposed by Russian, European, and American envoys.

BLACK SKY

In southeast Asia, the sky was again painted black by smog from burning forests in Indonesia. Last year the smog clouds reached Singapore and Malaysia causing widespread sickness.

KASHMIR CONFLICT FLARES UP

Indian aircraft attack guerrillas operating out of Kashmir on the Indian side and two aircraft are lost. India accuses the Pakistani army of supplying military equipment to the guerrillas. The two countries have fought a war over this territory on two previous occasions. By June, tension reaches its highest level for 30 years. India's prime minister, Atal Behari Vajpayee, says the campaign will continue until the infiltrators are driven out.

THE POPE IS BANNED

Pope John Paul is banned by China from visiting Hong Kong during his Asian tour because of the Vatican's ties with Taiwan. The pope still intends to visit the mainland via Macau.

A SOLAR ECLIPSE

Millions of onlookers watch the path of a solar eclipse as it passes over Europe, the Middle East, and Asia. By watching this natural phenomenon, many are anxious to dispel the idea that it is a precursor to an apocalypse as the century draws to an end.

BELOW: Izmit, Turkey is hit by an earthquake measuring 7.4 on the Richter scale. Rescue operations become a race against time as air runs out for survivors trapped under collapsed buildings.

RELENTLESS RAINS AND FLOODING

Rivers in the Ganges, Brahmaputra and Meghna basins overflow displacing nearly one million people as seasonal rains fall relentlessly in Bangladesh. Meanwhile in China, emergency workers battle to contain the flow of water from the Yangtze river and its tributaries. The water has been rising since June and by August, fed by tropical storm Olga, an estimated 1.8 million people are forced to move from the flooded plains in central and east China.

GREENPEACE FROZEN OUT

British Nuclear Fuels secure a Dutch court order to freeze Greenpeace's international bank account after arguing that the organization's protests caused extensive delays in preparing two controversial shipments of reprocessed plutonium to be shipped from France back to Japan. Both Britain and France had banned Greenpeace vessels from their waters. Greenpeace argues that the 20 tons of plutonium is a dangerous shipment.

ANC LANDSLIDE

The African National Congress wins almost two thirds of the vote in South Africa's second non-racial election, in June. It falls one seat short of a two-thirds majority in parliament. The ANC forms a coalition with the Inkatha Freedom Party giving a combined majority of more than three to one.

TURKEY EARTHQUAKE

The industrial northwest of Turkey is struck by a massive earthquake. The town of Izmit is the focus of destruction. Over 13,000 people are missing, many of them buried in shoddily constructed apartment blocks. A hospital and a military base are destroyed. An oil refinery erupts in fire. The government is criticized for contributing to a feeble rescue effort as international organizations dig for survivors. More than 200,000 people are now homeless as a result of the devastation. Three months later, in November, a second big earthquake hits a town 120 miles west of Ankara, the capital. Over 500 people are killed.

DEATH WISH GRANTED

Plans to legalize euthanasia and doctor-assisted suicide are published by the Dutch government. This action formalizes practices already carried out and accepted in the country. Working to very strict guidelines, children as young as 12 would be entitled to request death. If approved, The Netherlands will become the first country in the world to legalize mercy killings.

WORLD CHAMPIONS AGAIN

The New York Yankees won their third World Series in four years behind a strong pitching performance by veteran Roger Clemens. The Yankees defeated the Atlanta Braves in four straight games and have now won twelve consecutive World Series games.

ABOVE: Laptop computers and portable telephones are two of the biggest contributions to the fast-paced lifestyle of the 1990s.

BLOOD MONEY

I.G. Farben was the world's largest chemical company during World War II. One of its subsidiaries produced the lethal gases that were used to kill camp inmates in Nazi Germany. In August, more than 50 years after the end of the war, the shareholders agree to establish a $1.6 million fund to compensate former slave laborers. The move fails to satisfy survivor groups who are demanding an estimated $15 million and liquidating the company's assets which will be distributed to the victims.

COLD WAR REVISITED

An American congressional committee reveals that China has stolen classified information on numerous deployed warheads in their missile system. The spying had gone on for more that 20 years at Los Alamos National Laboratory in New Mexico. The U.S. government promises to tighten security at all government laboratories.

BACK TO TIANANMEN SQUARE

Ten years after the killings in Tiananman Square, China prepares for the anniversary by closing foreign satellite TV channels and blocking the internet. In an unprecedented legal action, the relatives of some of the victims in the original demonstration submit evidence to a Chinese court demanding a criminal investigation into the role played by officials and troops at the time.

PAKISTAN COUP

In mid-October, Pakistan's army overthrows Nawaz Sharif's government after it tries to remove General Pervez Musharraf from the top military position. Troops capture Sharif and gain control of the airports and TV stations as the General promises to maintain stability. Governments all over the world condemn the coup. The Commonwealth suspends Pakistan when the country's constitution is revoked.

ABOVE: The newly constructed interior of the Reichstag building sees the first full session of the Bundestag in April, as government power returns to Germany's historic capital.

RUSSIA DEFENDS ITS SOVEREIGNTY

In September, after more than three weeks of Russian artillery and air strikes, the guerrillas who invaded Dagastan are forced back into Chechnya in southern Russia. 30,000 soldiers are sent to Russia's border with Chechnya whose Islamic militants are accused of recent civilian bombings. Air attacks begin against what the Kremlin describes as terrorist targets. In November, it is estimated that over 180,000 Chechen civilians have fled their homes. By December, Russian ground forces in Chechnya enter the capital city of Grozny and begin fighting a dirty war of retribution.

JAPAN'S WOMEN COME LAST

Women in Japan finally get access to the birth control pill four decades after their counterparts in other industrialized countries. In contrast, it took just six months for the male dominated Japanese society to approve the sale of Viagra, the popular anti-impotence drug.

BATTERED BY FLOYD

More than 3.5 million people move out of the path of Hurricane Floyd as it works its way up the eastern coast of the U.S. States of emergency are declared in several states as the country's largest evacuation in history begins. Florida and Georgia are declared disaster areas.

HAPPY BIRTHDAY?

China celebrates 50 years of communism. An edition of *Time* magazine, which contains articles on human rights violations in China, is banned. The Chinese authorities crack down on the banned Falun Gong movement which said to have more adherents than China's Communist Party. It is accused of being superstitious, evil thinking, and an organization that sabotages social stability. Government agencies arrest unknown numbers of followers in security sweeps across Beijing after a silent protest was held in Tiananmen Square by supporters of the movement.

BELOW: Hurricane Floyd over the States. This weather satellite image helps to predict the possible path of damage. Flooding affects more than 200,000 people in the U.S. and even more in Central America.

Hurricane Floyd
GOES-8 Colorized IR Image

ABOVE: By the end of 1999, use of the electronic World Wide Web and the Internet leads to the computer becoming a household tool for communications and day-to-day activities.

WALL REMEMBERED

Germans and other Europeans celebrate the 10th anniversary of the fall of the Berlin Wall. At the same time, prison sentences given to East Germany's 1989 head of state, Egon Krenz, and other top communists who oversaw the shooting of possible escapees to the West, are upheld on appeal.

SUPER SIZED POPULATION

The Center for Disease Control and Prevention publishes a study which concludes that nearly 20 per cent of Americans are obese and that one in two adults are overweight.

ASSASSINATION

Five men gun down Armenia's Prime Minister Vazgen Sarkisian and seven other officials in the parliamentary chamber. The attack is caught on television and stuns the world. The gunmen take dozens of hostages, but surrender after a 12 hour siege. Their leader accuses the government of letting the country disintegrate and of rampant corruption.

PANAMA CANAL HANDED OVER

Control of the Panama Canal was given to Panama by a delegation headed by former President Jimmy Carter. Completed in 1914 at a cost of over $375 million, the route cut in half the sailing distance between New York City and San Francisco. Over 14,000 ships pass through the canal annually paying over $500 million in tolls.

CHINA ROCKETS INTO ORBIT

China successfully launches its first spacecraft and becomes only the third country, after the former Soviet Union and America, to develop and launch a space vehicle capable of carrying a person into space.

BRITISH-IRISH COUNCIL MEET

The momentum of the peace process in Northern Ireland is maintained in December at the first meeting of the British-Irish Council held in London. The Council was a result of the Good Friday Agreement.

INDEPENDENCE FIGHT

In Dili, East Timor, as the August 30 referendum draws near, anti-independence thugs launch attacks on the U.N. and pro-independence groups. By September 1, the militias go on a rampage. Most East Timorese vote for independence, but the violence continues to escalate during September. It is eventually brought under control by United Nation forces led by Australia. More than 300,000 Timorese have been left homeless in an effort to escape attack by the rampaging mobs. Indonesia subsequently cancels a four-year-old security agreement with Australia in protest to its actions.

BATTLE IN SEATTLE

World Trade Organization talks in Seattle face violent demonstrations not seen in America since the seventies. Protesters accuse the industrialized countries of placing the interests of international corporations before worker's rights and the environment. Damages exceed $2 million, over 500 people are arrested, and the trade talks collapse.

BERLIN AGREES TO COMPENSATION

Germany finally agrees to pay over $7 billion to survivors forced to work in German factories by the Nazis. The government and certain industries that exploited the citizens will equally finance the fund which will be dispersed to the victims. Almost 12 million people were forced to serve the Nazi war effort.

GATES DONATES

Microsoft founder Bill Gates has donated $26 million to UNICEF to fight maternal and neonatal tetanus.

MUDSLIDES KILL 30,000

The Venezuelan coastal state of Vargas is devastated by flooding and mudslides caused by torrential rain. The International Red Cross estimates that as many as 30,000 people have perished in the worst natural disaster to ever strike this country.

YELTSIN RESIGNS

In a surprise announcement, Boris Yeltsin resigns as Russia's president on New Year's Eve amid speculation that he has secured a deal to suppress corruption allegations against him concerning his years in power.

PARTY TIMES

From the International Date Line, in the Pacific Ocean, the midnight deadline spreads inexorably west. Millennium Island and Kiribati start the fireworks and are followed by spectacular displays in Auckland and Sydney. In China, fires light the Great Wall from end to end. In the desert of Africa, Timbuktu celebrates in the same spirit as ice-bound Anchorage in Alaska. The world parties in expectation: at the start of the 20th century, the life expectancy for a woman was 40 years, 100 years later it has doubled and the population stands at six billion. In non-industrialized nations, there remains over 2 billion people still without electricity and even more with no sanitation. Thus, the 21st century begins.

BELOW: Midnight, the final moment of the second Millennium, over Southampton Water, England.

1 9 9 9 ⟶ 2 0 0 0

ABOVE: The London Eye is a giant ferris wheel that fails to make its deadline. Built to herald the new millennium, it was bedevilled by safety problems. The Millennium Dome, however, also on the banks of the Thames, is completed just in time and is the focus of the capital's effort to welcome in the New Year. It stages exhibitions and performances designed to attract visitors.

LEFT: Jan. 1, 2000, daybreak in Tongan waters in the Pacific Ocean. To the west, the rest of the world awaits the midnight hour to start celebrations, as these islanders begin their day.

RIGHT: In West Beijing, revellers at the newly built China Century Monument, designed in the style of the Temple of Heaven used by Chinese emperors to perform major ceremonial rites, express their joy as the century turns.

ABOVE: At Sydney's Harbour Bridge and Opera House, one million people watch 22 tons of fireworks light the midnight sky.

ABOVE: In Jerusalem, fireworks explode over the Church of Nativity, the traditional birthplace of Jesus, in Manger Square, Bethlehem.

Pictured is Berlin's Brandenberg Gate during Germany's festivities. Over a million are estimated to join the all-night party in this historic district.

ABOVE LEFT: In Moscow, as their president resigns, a boy gazes into the future as he watches the new century sky above Red Square.
ABOVE RIGHT: Dubrovnik, the ancient Croatian city, draws thousands into the main square to celebrate. CNN announces that the city is in its top ten places in the world to celebrate the New Year 2000.

BELOW: In Rio de Janeiro, Copacabana beach hosts 100,000s of partygoers spectacularly welcoming the New Year and the 500th anniversary of the founding of Brazil.

ABOVE: Pope John Paul II watches the fireworks from his balcony at the Vatican at the start of the Christian third millennium. His message to followers is one of joy and peace.

London welcomes in the new millennium. The River Thames and the Houses of Parliament are reflected in the light of fireworks as the river is lit by a 'wall of fire'. Thousands pack the riverbanks to watch the display.

ABOVE: Paris, by popular vote, is the most visually stunning event in Europe. Fireworks burst from the Eiffel Tower as millions party on the boulevards by night.

In Sarajevo, Bosnians see in the New Year close to the National Theatre lit against a background of exploding fireworks after years of war in the 1990s.

BELOW: Two million gather in New York City to toast the New Year. Times Square is the traditional backdrop for the waving and cheering crowd as confetti rains down on them and fireworks explode.

In Toronto, a beautiful waterfront fireworks show rises from barges moored on Lake Ontario as Canadians join the celebrations twelve hours after they started to the east.

WINNERS AND ACHIEVERS OF THE 1990s

ACADEMY AWARDS

The Academy of Motion Picture Arts and Sciences was founded in 1927 by the movie industry to honor its artists and craftsmen. All categories of motion picture endeavor are honored, but the most significant are listed below.

BEST ACTOR

1990 Jeremy Irons *Reversal of Fortune*
1991 Anthony Hopkins *The Silence of the Lambs*
1992 Al Pacino *Scent of a Woman*
1993 Tom Hanks *Philadelphia*
1994 Tom Hanks *Forrest Gump*
1995 Nicolas Cage *Leaving Las Vegas*
1996 Geoffrey Rush *Shine*
1997 Jack Nicholson *As Good As It Gets*
1998 Roberto Benigni *Life is Beautiful*
1999 Kevin Spacey *American Beauty*

BEST ACTRESS

1990 Kathy Bates *Misery*
1991 Jodie Foster *The Silence of the Lambs*
1992 Emma Thompson *Howards End*
1993 Holly Hunter *The Piano*
1994 Jessica Lange *Blue Sky*
1995 Susan Sarandon *Dead Man Walking*
1996 Francis McDormand *Fargo*
1997 Helen Hunt *As Good As It Gets*
1998 Gwyneth Paltrow *Shakespeare in Love*
1999 Hilary Swank *Boy's Don't Cry*

BEST DIRECTOR

1990 Kevin Costner *Dances with Wolves*
1991 Jonathan Demme *The Silence of the Lambs*
1992 Clint Eastwood *Unforgiven*
1993 Steven Spielberg *Schindler's List*
1994 Robert Zemeckis *Forrest Gump*
1995 Mel Gibson *Braveheart*
1996 Anthony Minghella *The English Patient*
1997 James Cameron *Titanic*
1998 Steven Spielberg *Saving Private Ryan*
1999 Sam Mendes *American Beauty*

BEST PICTURE

1990 *Dances with Wolves*
1991 *The Silence of the Lambs*
1992 *Unforgiven*
1993 *Schindler's List*
1994 *Forrest Gump*
1995 *Braveheart*
1996 *The English Patient*
1997 *Titanic*
1998 *Shakespeare in Love*
1999 *American Beauty*

NOBEL PRIZES

The Nobel Prizes are an international award granted in the fields of literature, physics, chemistry, physiology or medicine, and peace. The first prizes were awarded in 1901 and funded by the money left in the will of the Swedish inventor Alfred Nobel (1833–1896), who gave the world dynamite.

PRIZES FOR LITERATURE

1990 Octavio Paz (Mexican) for poetry and essays
1991 Nadine Gordimer (South African) for fiction
1992 Derek Walcott (St Lucian-born) for poetry
1993 Toni Morrison (American) for fiction
1994 Kenzaburo Oe (Japanese) for fiction
1995 Seamus Heaney (Irish) for poetry
1996 Wislawa Szymborska (Poland) for poetry
1997 Dario Fo (Italian) for drama
1998 José Saramago (Portuguese) for fiction
1999 Gunter Grass (Germany) for non-fiction

PRIZES FOR PEACE

1990 Mikhail Gorbachev (Soviet) for promoting world peace
1991 Aung San Suu Kyi (Burmese) for non-violent struggle for democracy and human rights in Burma.
1992 Rigoberta Menchu (Guatemalan) for work to gain respect for the rights of Guatemala's Native Americans.
1993 Nelson Mandela and FW de Klerk (South African) for helping to integrate South Africa
1994 Yasser Arafat (Palestinian), Yitzhak Rabin (Israeli) and Shimon Peres (Israeli) for helping to promote Palestinian self-rule
1995 The organization known as the Pugwash Conference on Science and World Affairs and its president, Joseph Rotblat (British), for their efforts to eliminate nuclear weapons
1996 Carlos Ximenes Belo (Timorese) and Jose Ramos-Horta (Timorese) for their work on behalf of the people of East Timor
1997 Jody Williams (American) and the International Campaign to Ban Land Mines for work campaigning to defuse landmines
1998 John Hume and David Trimble for efforts to find a peaceful solution to the conflict in Northern Ireland
1999 Doctors Without Borders for the organization's humanitarian work on several continents

PRIZES FOR PHYSICS

1990 Jerome Friedman and Henry Kendall (American) and Richard Taylor (Canadian) for experiments proving the existence of subatomic particles called quarks
1991 Pierre-Gilles de Gennes (French) for analyses of alignments and other orderly arrangements of molecules in certain substances
1992 Georges Charpak (French) for the invention of devices that detect subatomic particles in particle accelerators
1993 Russell Hulse and Joseph Taylor, Jr. (American) for discovering dense pairs of stars called binary pulsars.
1994 Clifford Shull (American) and Bertram Brockhouse (Canadian) for developing neutron scattering as a technique for revealing the structure of matter
1995 Martin Perl (American) for research on a subatomic particle called the tau, and Frederick Reines (American) for the discovery of a subatomic particle called the neutrino.
1996 David M. Lee, Robert C. Richardson, and Douglas D. Osheroff (American) for discovering that a type of helium called helium-3 becomes a superfluid, a rare form of matter, at an extremely low temperature
1997 Steven Chu and William Phillips (American) and Claude Cohen-Tannoudji (French) for methods of investigation using laser light to cool and trap atoms
1998 Robert B. Laughlin (American) and Horst L. Stormer (German-born) and David C. Tsui (Chinese-born) for the discovery of a new form of quantum fluid with fractionally charged excitations
1999 Gerardus 't Hooft and Martinus J.G. Veltman (Dutch) for work on the quantum structure of electroweak interactions in physics

PRIZES FOR CHEMISTRY

1990 Elias James Corey (American) for artificially duplicating natural substances as compounds for use in drugs
1991 Richard Ernst (Swiss) for improvements in the use of nuclear magnetic resonance (NMR) to analyze chemicals
1992 Rudolph Marcus (American) for analyzing the transfer of electrons between molecules

1993 Michael Smith (Canadian) and Kary Mullis (American) for devising methods that made possible gene therapy, detection of the AIDS virus and multiplication of fossil DNA
1994 George Olah (American) for work on hydrocarbon molecules
1995 Mario Molina and F. Sherwood Rowland (American) and Paul Crutzen (Dutch) for work leading to the discovery of a "hole" in the earth's protective layer of ozone
1996 Richard E. Smalley and Robert Curl, Jr. (American) and Sir Harold W. Kroto (British) for discovering carbon molecules called fullerenes
1997 Jens Skou (Danish) for showing that enzymes can promote the movement of substances through a cell membrane; and John Walker (British) and Paul Boyer (American) for discoveries about adenosine triphosphate (ATP), a molecule that living things use to store energy
1998 Walter Kohn for the development of the density-functional theory; and John A. Pople (American) for the development of computational methods in quantum chemistry.
1999 Ahmad Zewail (Egyptian) for work making it possible to watch atoms in slow motion during incredibly fast chemical reactions

PRIZES FOR PHYSIOLOGY OR MEDICINE

1990 Joseph E. Murray and E. Donnall Thomas (American) for work in transplanting human organs and bone marrow
1991 Erwin Neher and Bert Sakmann (German) for discovering how cells communicate with one another
1992 Edmond Fischer and Edwin Krebs (American) for discovering a chemical process in cells that is linked to cancer and to rejection of transplanted organs
1993 Richard Roberts (British-born) and Phillip Sharp (American) for their discoveries about the structure and function of genes

1994 Alfred Gilman and Martin Rodbell (Americans) for discovering G-proteins
1995 Edward B. Lewis and Eric Wieschaus (American) and Christiane Nuesslein-Volhard (German) for studies of how genes control early embryo development
1996 Peter C. Doherty (Australian) and Rolf M. Zinkernagel (Swiss) for discovering the signals that alert white blood cells to kill virus-infected cells
1997 Stanley Prusiner (American) for a theory on prions, a class of infectious proteins found in brain disorders
1998 Robert F. Furchgott, Louis J. Ignarro and Ferid Murad (American) for discoveries concerning nitric oxide as a signalling molecule in the cardiovascular system
1999 Gunter Blobel (Germany) for his discovery that proteins have intrinsic signals that govern their transport

INDIANAPOLIS 500
1990 Arie Luyendyk
1991 Rick Mears
1992 Al Unser, Jr.
1993 Emerson Fittipaldi
1994 Al Unser, Jr.
1995 Jacques Villeneuve
1996 Buddy Lazier
1997 Arie Luyendyk
1998 Eddie Cheever
1999 Kenny Brack

KENTUCKY DERBY
1990 Unbridled
1991 Strike The Gold
1992 Lil E. Tee
1993 Sea Hero
1994 Go For Gin
1995 Thunder Gulch
1996 Grindstone
1997 Silver Charm
1998 Real Quiet
1999 Charismatic

NBA CHAMPIONS
1990 Detroit Pistons defeat Portland Trail Blazers
1991 Chicago Bulls defeat Los Angeles Lakers
1992 Chicago Bulls defeat Portland Trail Blazers
1993 Chicago Bulls defeat Phoenix Suns
1994 Houston Rockets defeat New York Knicks
1995 Houston Rockets defeat Orlando Magic
1996 Chicago Bulls defeat Seattle SuperSonics
1997 Chicago Bulls defeat Utah Jazz
1998 Chicago Bulls defeat Utah Jazz
1999 San Antonio Spurs defeat New York Knicks

SITES OF THE OLYMPIC GAMES
1992 SUMMER Barcelona, Spain
WINTER Albertville, France
1994 WINTER Lillehammer, Norway
1996 SUMMER Atlanta, USA
1998 WINTER Nagano, Japan
2000 SUMMER Sydney, Australia

U.S. PRESIDENTS
1989–1993 President George Bush, *Republican*
1989–1993 Vice President Dan Quayle
1993–2000 President Bill Clinton, *Democrat*
1993–2000 Vice President Al Gore

SUPER BOWL CHAMPIONS
1990 San Francisco 49ers defeat Denver Broncos
1991 New York Giants defeat Buffalo Bills
1992 Washington Redskins defeat Buffalo Bills
1993 Dallas Cowboys defeat Buffalo Bills
1994 Dallas Cowboys defeat Buffalo Bills
1995 San Francisco 49ers defeat San Diego Chargers
1996 Dallas Cowboys defeat Pittsburgh Steelers
1997 Green Bay Packers defeat New England Patriots
1998 Denver Broncos defeat Green Bay Packers

1999 Denver Broncos defeat Atlanta Falcons

WORLD CUP FINAL MATCHES

YEAR	LOCATION
1990	**Rome**

West Germany defeats Argentina 1-0
1994 **Pasadena**
Brazil 0 Italy 0
Brazil wins 3–2 on penalty kicks.
1998 **Paris**
France defeats Brazil 3-0

WIMBLEDON CHAMPIONS
1990 MEN Stefan Edberg
WOMEN Martina Navratilova
1991 MEN Michael Stitch
WOMEN Steffi Graf
1992 MEN Andre Agassi
WOMEN Steffi Graf
1993 MEN Pete Sampras
WOMEN Steffi Graf
1994 MEN Pete Sampras
WOMEN Conchita Martinez
1995 MEN Pete Sampras
WOMEN Steffi Graf
1996 MEN Richard Krajicek
WOMEN Steffi Graf
1997 MEN Pete Sampras
WOMEN Martina Hingis
1998 MEN Pete Sampras
WOMEN Jana Novotna
1999 MEN Pete Sampras
WOMEN Lindsay Davenport

WORLD SERIES CHAMPIONS
1990 Cincinnati Reds defeat Oakland Athletics
1991 Minnesota Twins defeat Atlanta Braves
1992 Toronto Blue Jays defeat Atlanta Braves
1993 Toronto Blue Jays defeat Philadelphia Phillies
1994 *Not played due to strike*
1995 Atlanta Braves defeat Cleveland Indians
1996 New York Yankees defeat Atlanta Braves
1997 Florida Marlins defeat Cleveland Indians
1998 New York Yankees defeat San Diego Padres
1999 New York Yankees defeat Atlanta Braves